I0103595

Nathaniel R. Middleton

The allegory of Plato and other essays

Nathaniel R. Middleton

The allegory of Plato and other essays

ISBN/EAN: 9783743377301

Manufactured in Europe, USA, Canada, Australia, Japa

Cover: Foto ©Thomas Meinert / pixelio.de

Manufactured and distributed by brebook publishing software
(www.brebook.com)

Nathaniel R. Middleton

The allegory of Plato and other essays

THE ALLEGORY OF PLATO

AND OTHER ESSAYS IN

PROSE AND VERSE

By N. RUSSELL MIDDLETON, L.L. D.

EDITED BY HIS SON,

N. R. MIDDLETON, Jr.

CHARLESTON, S. C.
WALKER, EVANS & COGSWELL COMPANY, PUBLISHERS,
3 and 5 Broad and 117 East Bay Streets.
1891.

THE ALLEGORY OF PLATO.

Νοήματα επι την ζωην.

N his thesis of Life the great thinker of old,
Adopted a metaphor striking and bold ;
And in view of that two-fold phenomenon man
It is thus that his mental philosophy ran.
The moral probationer ruling on earth,
In two opposite courses is drawn from his birth.
On the one hand he strives like a steed all on fire,
To spurn his gross nature and upward aspire ;
The other a dull and inanimate clod,
Contented with labor and bound to the sod.
For the term of probation, the brief span of life,
These horses are yoked in perpetual strife ;
And the steed we select as our emblem below,
Shall rule us forever for weal or for woe.

Far back in the morning of time as he wrote,
The vision of Plato, prophetic of thought,
Appealed to the versatile mind of the Greek,
Accustomed in fanciful figure to speak;
But the truth he enclosed in that mystical shell
Touched more than the ear of the Greek as it fell;
And the salient thought of each secular age
Responds to the thought of the Attican sage;
For vice stalks abroad in the eye of the day,
And the autumn winds whisper of death and decay,
And there comes to the soul in its moments of bliss
A vision of life that is nobler than this,
When, spurning this region of doubt and dispute
We rest in the infinite—awe-struck and mute.

There is power in sense, there is beauty on earth,
And the universe teems with a wonderful birth;
From the plains to the mountains, o'er valley and hill
Love glows in the sunshine and laughs in the rill.
And the mind which has yielded to reason's control,
Finds God in creation and light in his soul:
But sense is a traitor and panders to vice,
Now heated to phrensy, now colder than ice;

All smiles to the world, but a tyrant within,
It mocks at the fool it has led into sin ;
And the madman who trusts it still finds to his cost
His happiness wrecked and his nobleness lost ;
The black horse of Plato, his eye downward cast,
To earth and to earthliness riveted fast,
The blue ether above, the pure mirror of hope
Forever revealing and giving it scope,
The stars and the sunset, the rainbow on high,
Never gild the horizon of that loveless eye,
For dead to all beauty, concentered in self,
Overpowered by lust or hoodwinked by pelf,
The probationer charged with a heaven-bound soul,
Learns to browse with the ox or to grope with the
    mole ;
And when the great Landlord who lent him his
    powers,
Comes to reckon and weigh those parturient hours,
And naught but the mouse of the fable is born,
What is left to the hapless pretender but scorn ?

There is joy in Ambition, a glorified sense,
More pure than the palate, more potent than pence,

To expand in the sunshine and conscious of power,
To feel that we govern the thought of the hour,
To scale Matterhorn the majestic and view
Creation beneath us a moment or two;
It may be a folly, but folly sublime
And the heart will exult in that soul-stirring time,
And forgetting the shortness, delusion and pain
Will nurse the wild hope that its joy will remain.
It is true we are warned by the laboring breath
And the blast of the storm in that region of death,
But fame is a recompense dearer than life,
And the blare of her trumpet inspirits the strife,
And the shouts of the thousands who see us ascend
Shall waken an echo that never shall end;
Though the bones of precursors are bleaching
      around,
Or lie buried beneath in the crevasse profound,
Though the avalanche thunder its warning afar,
And the mist of the mountain obscure every star,
Though the company falter and faint one by one
And the guide, now discouraged, is with us alone,
On the pinnacled peak human feet never pressed,
We will plant our flag and to fate leave the rest;

And the world of to-day and the thousands unborn,
Shall hail us the victors of proud Matterhorn.
But victor and triumph, phenomenal both,
Only live to fulfil that primordial oath
That Time and its contents, unreal alike,
Shall cease when the watchman his tocsin shall strike,
Like the mist of the mountain shall vanish away
With all that we cling to as real to-day.

It is charged by the thoughtless, denied by the few,
That what the great Berkley affirmed was untrue;
His science was folly, philosophy blind
And to prove it the skeptic appealed to mankind.
Shall the earth, such a solid material ball,
Its mountains and vallies, its forests and all,
Shall the Earth melt away like a dream that is past
Or a garment outworn and discarded at last?
Is not matter eternal? Can aught lose its place
In the organized forms of unlimited space?
But what are those forms? And what is that space?
And what the distinctions of genus and race?
And what the strong arm, the contemplative brow
And the eye which compels all creation to bow?

Phenomenal all, but the breath of the Lord,
The outspoken birth of his creative word.
Creative forever, creative perforce,
No beginning, no end to that infinite course;
We may talk of the atoms in which it began,
Or reduce to its monads the infinite plan,
But atoms or monads, or molecules or cells
'Tis the *Lord of Creation* within them that dwells,
And when force in the mind of the dwelling attain
The force of the Architect once to explain
Let *Existence* work out in its thought if it can
The *Essence* of power in which it began.
Oh! impotent man, doomed forever to kick
'Gainst the pricks and without needed straw to make
          brick,
Oh! man, deign for once thy true lot to accept
Nor, created a tyro, still ape the adept.

Ambition! Oh yes, when it bids us arise
And on wings of humility soar to the skies,
Ambition! when duty unflinching and stern
A pure vestal fire unceasing shall burn,

But when like the poet whose marvellous lyre
Was nursed by a genius a God might inspire,
It visits the earth but to scorch and to blight
And dazzle the nations with wildfire light,
The soul of the man all concentered within
Though gifted and great has no safeguard from sin,
And that comet like genius portentous and rare,
To the spirit of wisdom suggestive of fear,
Its mission soon ended, world-worshiped no more,
Its place in the sky shall be void as before.

And so, when that idol of national pride
Who swept like a meteor over the tide
Whose watchword was *duty*, whose war cry *advance*
Whose trophies the blockaded navies of France;
From his cenotaph rest 'neath the dome of St. Paul,
On the world for its envied approval shall call,
Let the voice of the injured be heard in reply,
And the protest of Virtue ascend to the sky.
Shall the poor honest sailor who hung on his word
Whose soul by the watchword of *duty* was stirred
Be reminded by him of the motto engraved
On the flag of his country wherever it waved?

Shall he prate of *Duty* who, living for fame,
Spurned the first of all duties, to home and to name ?
Shall he talk of *Honor*, her foe and her bane
Who living has taken her great name in vain ?
Shall he challenge Glory whose dying bequest
Consigned to his country a shameful request ?
The defender of England from external foe,
Who dealt her at home a far deadlier blow
Than if Europe combined in invidious might
Against her renown had assembled in fight.
When the sacredest ties have been brought to an end,
Oh ! tell, if thou canst, what is left to defend ?
When the homes of old England no longer are pure,
And her tender relations no longer secure,
Let the joy-loving Celt his gay system advance,
And Britain learn morals from Rousseau and France.

Ambition ! oh yes, when the good of the State
And millions shall look to one man for their fate,
Who, leaving the bliss of domestic repose,
Assumes the control with its pilloried woes,
Like Vasa, of old, his conditions demand,
And acting the despot, enfranchise the land.

No country need dread such ambition as this,
No statesman look higher for national bliss ;
Ambition that plunders, ambition that raves,
Whose way-marks are ruins, whose trophies are
    graves,
The aim of whose being is selfish renown,
Who rises alone because others are down,
Who still with the *relative* rises or sinks,
Dares only to think as the multitude thinks ;
Such a soul may survive for an hour or so
But the touch of the *Real* will hurl it below,
Below where the agents of Tyranny dwell,
And if it must reign, reign sublimely in Hell.

Society claims from each member her rights
And offers to each her unchallenged delights ;
In the fair social circle mind offers to mind
A stimulus healty, robust and refined ;
There is room for the brilliant encounter of wits,
To catch the aroma of life as it flits,
To receive and return, when deprived of its barb,
The arrow concealed under ridicule's garb,

To encourage, invite and call into play
The thoughts which inform and embellish the day,
To raise the desponding and comfort the sad,
To nourish with oil and with wine to make glad.
The Power that made us and placed us on earth
Ever values the soul by its fair social worth;
And this is the question that seals every lot,
Is his role in society noble or not?
But society shares the defects of the race,
And its members alas! never know their own
        place;
The adroit and unscrupulous oft' fill the seat
From which modest merit is forced to retreat,
And fools in their folly attempt without dread
To enter where angels with diffidence tread,
A world of confusion, a world out of gear,
Now goaded to madness, now crouching in fear,
All drunk with the blood of her martyrs to-day,
And chanting to-morrow a soft roundelay;
Her honor degraded, her standard debased,
Her temple in ruins, her altars displaced.
When her morals are based on the Code of *Sin-john*,
And the type which she models her manners upon

Is the mask of a Chesterfield, hollow and false,
And her maidens surrender their charms to the valse,
And the harvest which springs from the desolate land
Is polluted with tares from Duke Rochefoucauld's
      hand,
Her dignity, purity, honor forgot,
The dark horse of Plato prefigures her lot.

But high on the mountains behold him advance,
The Knight of the Red Cross, with shield and with
      lance,
His loins girt with " *truth* " and bright o'er his head,
Her banner in stainless allegiance outspread ;
His breastplate of "*Righteousness*" shielded by "*faith*"
As the law of his holy knight-errantry saith,
His *Sandals* conformed to the same potent *word*
Which bound to his thigh his keen two-edged sword.
The knight of the Red-Cross rides on in his might
In armor resplendent, equipped for the fight,
His feet with the blood of his enemies red
And *Salvation* inscribed on his helmeted head.
The Knight of the Red-Cross ! Ye ages declare
How his effigies still in succession appear ;

In the mirror of time how they pass in review
From Enoch the holy to Stonewall the true ;
How, released from the trammels of sense and of
     greed,
In lordly procession they answer earth's need,
And waving the sword of protection on high,
In humanity's cause swear to conquer or die ;
And in dying they conquer, for each leaves a name,
To rise like the Phœnix from ashes and flame :
And when on the field he surrenders his trust
His fellow succeeds ere it fall to the dust ;
And though in the thick of the fight as we stand,
And look vainly around for the rescuing hand,
Never doubt that his presence is still on the earth
Awaiting, in hope, a miraculous birth :
Never doubt that the man and the martyr will rise
To drag to the sunlight each refuge of lies :
To expose the deceiver and awe the profane
And snatch from the lawless usurper his gain.

Trace backward the ages, in fancy unroll
The   records   which   live   in   the   world's   sacred
     scroll ;

On the Syrian plains see the fair Hebrew boy
Of his gray-headed sire the comfort and joy.
When the black cloud of envy unbound and enlarged
By the demon of hate was at length overcharged;
An exile from home, a stranger and slave,
Where the gray reeds of Nile in monotony wave,
The victim of lust, in his innocent youth
A prey to the passion that knoweth no ruth,
Still firm in his virtue though fiercely assailed
By the temptress that wooed and the tyrant that
    railed;
And thrust into prison midst felons and slaves,
Where villany rules and debauchery raves;
Ever true to the star that had guided his path,
Neither conquered by fear, nor excited by wrath,
Upheld by his conscience and cheered by his trust
In the final success of a cause that was just;
Never seeking distinction, nor dreaming of power,
Fulfilling in calmness the claims of the hour;
Exerting the gift of that mystical lore
Which on Syrian plains he had gathered of yore;
And bringing the stores of his wisdom to bear
On the sorrows and pains which abound everywhere

Unmoved by the sadness which fell to his lot
When ungrateful offenders their promise forgot;
Brought, at length, in the fulness of time, to the light,
With recompense, freedom and honor in sight,
Still nobly refused, by a tacit assent,
To appropriate power which only was lent;
And urged to display his miraculous art,
Thus bravely declined to assume a false part,
" The thing is not in me, my wisdom must cease,
God shall give Pharaoh an answer of peace."

But look once again upon history's page,
From the courage of youth to the wisdom of age.
See, armed with his rod on the sea-beaten strand,
The Hebrew law-giver in majesty stand;
No sword on his thigh, no crown on his brow,
The true man was simple and meek then as now;
While millions still trustingly bowed to his nod,
The leader himself humbly bowed to his God,
And while bearding the despot alone in his den,
The title he loved was " the meekest of men."
And thus, ever thus, in the record of life,
Though foremost in duty and bravest in strife,

The heart of the Hero expands to his Race,
And freely enlarges, the world to embrace ;
And poising a scepter or wielding a sword,
Overflows with the patience and love of his Lord.

But dwell not too long on the Mosaic page,
From the Prophet and Leader contemplate the sage ;
From thunder-scarped Sinai and Pisgah's proud head,
Descend to the prison where honesty bled.
From scenes that delight us and visions that please,
Let us gather in awe round the doomed Socrates ;
The healer of Athens diseased and in pain,
Who sought to restore her to virtue again,
Who lived for his country and, dying, refused
To question her laws though unjust and abused.
The foe of her tyrants, the friend of her youth,
Detector of fallacy, Lover of truth ;
Who greeted the death-laden cup with a smile
And yielded to envy a soul without guile.
In life's compensation 'twas fitting indeed,
That the man who alone his pure spirit could read,
Should give to the world his immaculate thought
And tell of the sorrow by which it was bought ;

2

'Twas meet that a Plato should rise to record
In diction superb, his oracular word ;
And Greece and the world understanding too late,
The secret significance wrapt in his fate,
Should hasten the deified martyr to greet
And in impotent shame cast their crowns at his feet.
Oh ! Athens, Oh Earth ever must it be so ?
That the great and the good must be scorned here
　　below ?
That the soul which is linked with the white-winged
　　steed
In its struggle for freedom must suffer and bleed ?
And the crown which on high the pure spirit adorns
Prove ever below a sharp crown of thorns?
Even so, ye far-seeing, self-conquering band
On the verge of two worlds who have taken your
　　stand,
And turning away from the transient, which fills
The eye of the world, to the infinite hills,
Count the Earth and its estimates lighter than straw
When compared with the vision that Socrates saw ;
That hint of the real, that glimpse of true life,
That kindles the soul and ennobles its strife ;

That from dust and delusion the neophite brings,
And bears him aloft on its tireless wings,
From tyrannous passion and sensuous love
To the freedom that reigneth and blesseth above.
Oh ! Earth and Oh ! Athens ! awakened too late,
Ye bend, all in vain, o'er the tomb of the Great.
All in vain ye have come, in remorse, on your knees,
To honor the shade of divine Socrates.

But think not in deserts and dungeons alone
There is purity found, it was found on a Throne ;
On the throne of the Cæsars, where gluttony raged,
And the war with mankind was so brutally waged ;
In the Palace where mortals assumed to be God,
And legalized villains audaciously trod ;
Whose denizens gloated o'er agonized throes,
Or complacently smiled at humanity's woes ;
Where tyrants were sacred and demons divine,
Hail the advent at length of beloved Antonine,
Imperial sage and philosopher saint,
A self-governed anchorite scorning restraint,
A law to himself, though raised above law,
A Father though hedged by traditional awe,

In virginal purity guarding his life
Where adultery raged and corruption was rife.
Let the misanthrope Dean who dishonored his race,
Who scoffed at their virtue and proved their disgrace,
Who took for his target an ideal man,
Constructed to suit his malevolent plan,
And raised on its pinnacled pedestal high,
To the foul-visaged image invited each eye ;
Let him blush when he reads in the records of time
The thoughts which have rendered the thinker sub-
  lime,
And veiling from sight his base caricature,
Make Marcus Aurelius his true cynosure.

In the morning of life when the earth was still young,
From lives of simplicity nobleness sprung ;
And men became great from a childlike repose
In the faith out of which all true greatness arose.
But time in its flight changed the thoughts of the hour,
And discord arose and the struggle for power,
And the Lords of the Earth and vicegerents of
  Heaven
Ceased to furnish mankind their appropriate leaven.

Thus power abused aroused protest and blame,
And close upon protest invective and shame ;
And the men of the world and the servants of God
Alike upon Honor and decency trod :
But while partisan passion must ever increase,
The spirit of *truth* is a spirit of peace ;
And while Luther upbraided and Leo cajoled,
One intelligent mind kept his faith as of old,
Whose wisdom the limits of liberty knew,
And left something still for his Maker to do.
In modesty shrinking from martyrdom's crown
He proved a true martyr without the renown ;
And standing alone on the fair neutral ground,
Kept his eye on the goal unto which he was bound.
Erasmus the learned, Erasmus the true,
Disowned by the powerful, loved by the few,
Who saw that his part was to scatter the seed,
To open the soil and root out the weed ;
The weed in man's nature, the passion and pride
Which tortured the soul of the friend at his side,
And that when his own work had been honestly
    done
The rest must be left to the rain and the sun,

Nor vainly and childishly look for in time
The fruit which matures in a healthier clime
But vain was his modesty, firmness and sense,
The cry was for violence, power and pence,
And calmness and wisdom were far out of place
In the turmoil and strife of a partisan race,
And the glory of christendom, type of true worth
On history's page made a subject of mirth,
On earth finds alone in some truth-loving breast
Intelligent sympathy, shelter and rest.
No comment is needed, his record will tell
If the verdict was just which from enemies fell,
And vindicate him whose integrity bore
The hatred of *Henry* and friendship of *More.*

Creation is *order*, each grade in its place
Gives assurance of harmony, beauty and grace;
But the petty distinctions we organize here,
Are unknown in the range of the heavenly sphere;
We lavish applause on the whims of the hour,
We glory in wealth and we idolize power;
And the statue that breathes, and the portrait that glows,
Soothe the heroes of Earth in their earthly repose;

But all are not heroes, her motherly breast
Earth opens to gather each child to his rest,
And each lies as tenderly watched over there,
As the saint in his tomb, or the King on his bier;
For the Father who loves—not the sinless alone—
Who yearns o'er his erring and prodigal son,
Hath a place in his heart and a seat at his board
For the child of his love whether peasant or lord;
And the pariah barred from the touch of his race,
Is welcomed by him to a filial embrace.

The heroes of Earth who monopolise fame,
Who lavish life's treasure to purchase a name;
Who live, all unconscious, on flattery's breath,
And shrink from desertion no less than from death:
The heroes of Earth have their day and are gone,
What they lived for has perished, or died for has flown;
Here a dynasty totters, a throne topples o'er
And rights, that men died for, are valued no more.
To escape from the doom that o'ershadowed their
      birth
Men make in their madness a Hell upon Earth;

And each earns a place in the Kingdom of Love
By hating below what is cherished above.
" *Audax omnia perpeti* " sang the poet of yore,
And " *ruit per nefas* " he sings evermore .
To do justly, love mercy, is childish control,
To walk humbly degrades an aspiring soul,
And he that wades deepest in blood of his race
Upon history's role holds the loftliest place.

Shall we linger in shadows that flit o'er the road ?
Shall we seek in the transient our chosen abode ?
Shall we claim as our kindred the brutes that we rule
And descend to the level of tiger and mule ?
While conscience within and the heavens above
Proclaim us the heirs of an infinite Love ?
Can immortal desires be fed with the fare
Which perishing natures contentedly share ?
And the life we inspire as our natural breath
Be quenched in the vapors mephitic of death
While we cherish a nature whose goal is the tomb
And bury the future in measureless gloom ?
No, the gentle and modest, the loving and true
Who live not for glory and claim not their due.

Who stand in their lot be it easy or hard,
Nor weakly betray what their honor should guard,
Who seek not to rest in an ignoble fame,
Nor tamper with conscience to purchase a name ;
Who build not on wealth the repose of the mind,
Nor measure their worth in the scales of mankind,
Who shun not the path which the martyrs have trod,
Nor ask recognition accept from their God ;
Who rejoice in the peace which obscurity brings,
And estimate lightly phenomenal things ;
These nurslings of Truth, who rest in her arms
And hide in her breast from all earthly alarms,
Cast pitying eyes from their sacred retreat
On the turmoil and strife of the world at their feet,
And soften the horrors of Time's lurid light
By the labors of love and the songs of the night.

On conditions we hold our tenure of life,
Conditions of agony, question and strife,
The good and the evil, the right and the wrong,
Are the tests of our manhood our journey along ;
But the weak and the timid, the selfish and vain
Shrink aghast from a struggle embittered by pain,

And the guerdon which conscience awards to the brave
Has no charms for a soul which is quenched in the
          grave,
The creatures of God as they came from his hand
Came each with a nature by Deity planned ;
And the welfare of each must be guaged by a law
Which meets the demands its Creator foresaw.
The *Immortal* demands an immortal supply—
The spirit seeks ever its guerdon on high ;
And the Prodigal, starved on the husks of the swine,
Yearns, thirstingly yearns for a banquet divine ;
A banquet which *Reason* and *Truth* shall provide
Where *Honor* shall rule and *Love* shall preside,
Whose servants shall call each appropriate guest
From the highways and hedges, the east and the west ;
A glorious band, the elect of the Earth,
Undistinguished by fame and unnoted by birth,
Whose heraldry boasts evangelical lore,
And whose lineage springs from the ranks of the poor ;
" *Ich dien* " their motto, a cross for their crest,
And their *order*, the flock that by Jesus was blest.
The Earth by their presence replenished, subdued,
Its beauty restored and its vigor renewed,

Its homesteads rejoicing in music and mirth,
No emigrant forced from the land of his birth,
Its valleys o'erflowing with corn and with wine,
Or greeting the ear with the lowing of kine,
Its "verdurous slopes" in fair contrast combine
The shade of the fig-tree and grace of the vine,
Where the infant shall play on the hole of the asp,
Or fondle the beast with innocuous clasp,
Where the wolf shall lie down in the fold with the
      lamb,
And the kid wander fearless unwatched by its dam ;
Where the Lion shall loathe his carnivorous prey,
And share with the ox his pure diet of hay ;
Where men shall unite, not to buttress the wrong,
Overawe the defenceless and bow to the strong,
But justice shall sit on the throne of the world,
And the ensigns of battle forever be furled ;
Where on God's holy mount none shall hurt or de-
      stroy,
But the welfare of all shall each member employ,
Where greed shall be outlawed and discord shall cease
And nature attain her Æonian peace.

RESPONSIBILITY.

I N the effort to analyse existence, I find that I reach my ultimatum in consciousness, and when I interrogate that, the answer, coming as it were with oracular power, seems to be on this wise, The whole of your existence is expressed in one word, Responsibility; For your creation and its attendant circumstances the responsibility rests with your Maker; as far as that is concerned you are both ignorant and impotent and therefore irresponsible, but for the preservation and development of your being the case is different, for these you have been furnished with adequate faculties and for these therefore you are responsible. It is in the due exercise of reason or the balancing power, that we learn to dispose aright of this question of responsibility, and keep the balance properly adjusted. If we assume responsibilities which do not belong to us we shall overtask ourselves and sink under the pressure; if we fail to meet our

responsibilities our faculties will deteriorate for want
of exercise and we shall lose our status in the order
of creation. It is important, then, to a rational agent,
first to establish a correct category of responsibilities
and then to dispose of the items in an orderly man-
ner. And first, I did not create myself. Consciousness testifies to this by affirming a state of perfectly
passive existence preceding any effort of either mental or physical power. My will was the consequent,
not the antecedent, of my existence. Nor is this all,
I not only did not create myself, but I was not per-
mitted to choose whether I would exist or not, and
the history of human life furnishes many a case in
which it has been shaken off as a burden too heavy to
be borne.

Again, I am not responsible for the circumstances
which attend me. That I am in a material world,
that my connection with this world involves action
and reaction, appropriation and rejection, identity and
antipathy, personality and community, individuality
and universality; that in one sense I am inseparably
united with my nature and in another wholly discon-
nected from her, and that out of this universal anti-

thetic duality grows apparent confusion, discordance
and incompatibility; for all this and the innumerable
resulting difficulties I am not in the smallest degree
responsible. If I had been left to myself I certainly
would not have introduced myself into a world
where my existence would necessarily involve struggle and my experience suffering; and as I was placed
in such circumstances without the concurrence of my
will, I unhesitatingly reject them from the category of
my responsibilities.

Neither am I responsible for my moral status, the
burden of morality with its attendant disabilities I
could never have voluntarily assumed, the paradoxes,
inconsistencies and impossibilities, which it seems to
imply, would have compelled me to decline an under-
taking manifestly beyond my strength. To be ushered into a garden of delights and warned that each
flower is a snare and each fruit a poison, that the
ground is charged with exhalations and the air laden
with death, that in this resplendent temple sits Circé
with her enchanted cup, and in yonder inviting garden
dwell the hesperides with their dragon-guarded
fruit; that in this bosky dell lurks the naiad to be-

guile me into the water, and on that sandy beach
roams the siren to lure me to the land; that west-
ward there are Scylla and Charybdis, and eastward
the clashing rocks; that in the north there is Medea
with her fiery enchantments, and in the south Medusa
with her basilisk glance ; that there are mœnades and
giants and harpies threatening me at every step of my
doubtful path ; this is no very inviting programme to
the traveller, conscious, as yet, of nothing but his own
ignorance and imbecility. It is well for us, my
friends, that you and I were not consulted when we
were sent into existence to meet such an ordeal as
this ; it is well for us that there has never been set
before us, in one appalling coup-d'œil, the incidents of
our unwonted journey ; it is well that the appoint-
ment was in another mind and the arrangement in
other hands.

Again, we are not responsible for the conduct of
others ; this is a very important item to be deducted
from the list of our mental burdens, which we are
constantly tempted to assume but which we have
neither the right nor the power to bear. We are all
conscious of secret uncontrollable misgivings as to

what may be said or done to our injury by enemies
and detractors; perhaps there is not one of our burdens which weighs upon us more heavily than this,
because it is limitless and undefined. In moments of
depression all nature seems against us, danger lurks
at every corner, disgrace is hovering over every path,
and the whole human race—our friends and brothers
—seem united in solid phalanx to obstruct our progress to honor and happiness. It is no trifling relief
to our overburdened nature to be assured that this is
all a delusion, that the wills we suspect are only free
subjectively, and the agents we dread are the instruments of a benignant power. A relief, and yet how
hard to realize! The assassins' dagger is a relentless
reality, the slanderer's venom is a poignant fact, no arm
of power intervenes, no voice of authority interposes
to avert the deadly blow; other lives and other charac-
ters have been at the mercy of the malignant and re-
vengeful, why not my own? Are not sensible facts
worth more than fanciful theories or metaphysical
myths? So reason the thoughtless multitude, so
reasoned the Ptolemaic astronomers. The revolution
of the sun is a sensible fact, the revolution of the

earth is a figment of the imagination ; he is a fool or a madman who would persuade us against the evidence of our senses. Yet science has verified the material paradox. When will a reasonable confidence in the integrity of our Maker convince us of the other?

Again, we are not responsible for the quality or the relative power of our faculties. One would think that it would be hardly necessary to enunciate such a proposition as this to beings endowed with common intelligence and a moral sense, and perhaps this may be true as far as the abstract statement is concerned, but our daily practice and our social experience sadly contradict the suggestions of reason in this, as in many other departments of human intercourse. We have been sent into the world with faculties, both mental and bodily, not only varying in every possible degree, but maturing with equal irregularity ; this arrangement is final and beyond dispute, and would seem to administer a severe rebuke to the struggles of human vanity and ambition, as well as a clear indication of the order of the universe as organized in the counsels of its divine originator ; according to

3

that organization, the value of the agent is established, not by any arbitrary standard involving private contests and personal rivalries, but by an absolute principle of adaptedness and an honest exercise of industry in the department for which the agent is especially provided; according to that absolute standard individual merit is dependent, as it should be, not upon accident or caprice, but upon circumstances wholly within the control of the agent himself; and, if he fail, there can be no question upon whom the blame should rest. Our Creator has not left us in a matter of such infinite moment at the disposal of any arbitrary or accidental influences, he has put our true dignity and our true honor wholly in our own hands.

Again, we are not responsible for temporal success. I do not mean to deny or even to question the temporal rewards of virtue, I do not mean to insinuate a doubt as to the inherent and universal and uncompromising distinction between good and evil, in every department of moral existence; but we must never forget that good and evil are relative distinctions and can have no possible place in the absolute appointments of a benevolent Creator; all those appointments must, from the necessity of the case, have reference to ultimate and eternal good, and to bring that about, evil which is temporary and relative, becomes as available and necessary an instrument in the divine hands as that more specious and acceptable form of mundane existence, which we, in our narrow and sensual estimates, pronounce to be good; poverty is an evil, disease is an evil, sorrow is an evil, sin is an evil, but it may be necessary for us to experience every one of these to ensure our attainment of ultimate and infinite good.

But enough of this, I am not attempting an exhaustive catalogue, wholly unnecessary in an address merely intended to be suggestive; let us leave the negative and take up the positive antithesis. I said that we were not responsible for the fact of existence. Is there not, nevertheless, an aspect in which our existence does involve responsibility? If we did not make ourselves are we not shut up to the conclusion that some one did make us? And are we not bound, as far as possible, as far at least as our attitude towards Him is concerned, to understand the being

who holds towards us this fundamental relationship,
constituted as we are a congeries of powers? Are
we not bound, in justice to ourselves, to discover the
nature and will of the being who organized those
powers and gave them unity and purpose? I do not
mean to trench upon the province of theology, I do
not mean to urge upon you any special views upon a
subject, which, if it be handled at all, should only be
touched with reverence and humility; I simply ask,
in reason and in common sense, if we are not bound
to know what can be known of the author of our
consciously responsible existence; and without any
reference to a higher claim, which has been made a
matter of infinite doubt and discussion, do we not
at least owe it to ourselves to settle a question upon
which our well being seems undeniably to rest? I
simply suggest the obligation because if you assent
to it sincerely there will be no difficulty in finding out
the way to meet it. A great thinker has maintained
that "the tap-root of every man's character is his
estimate of God" and it would not, I should think,
require much reflection to perceive that it is a matter
of infinite moment to us whether we regard our

Maker as a demon to be propitiated or a Father to be loved. What becomes of my human doubts and fears? What becomes of my fear of secret enmity or open violence if I am authorized to appropriate a divine paternity? "He need not dread created might who loves God the Creator." What becomes of my fear of death, my reluctance to meet visibly and face to face him whose companionship I have invoked, whose counsel I have sought, whose correction I have invited during this transitory obscuration of his presence? He is still the same unchangeable being whatever may be the vicissitudes of my probationary experience; let me only be assured that I have a filial claim upon his favor, and I cease to regard with personal anxiety the acts of any or all of his dependent creatures; and how is it possible for me to doubt the existence of such a claim when it stands avouched in the life and death of that divine man by whose earthly mission it was so clearly vindicated and proclaimed. But again, as we are responsible for a proper acquaintance with the Author of our being, so are we for our estimate of his work. The facts are all before us, the material creation enfolds us in its

universal embrace, we lie upon its bosom and it gives
us form and phenomenality; we act through it and
upon it and it constitutes, as far as we can judge, an
indispensable element of our individuality; it will
not do then to despise it, and the position of the
ascetic, the cynic and the stoic are all alike unnatural
and untenable. Grant that the body is but an instrument or manifestation of the mind; in either case we
are bound to secure its utmost availability and we are
plainly responsible for any failure, either personal or
relative, which may result from the neglect of its un-
deniable claims: but of course those claims are only
secondary; important as the instrument may be, it
cannot be placed upon the same level with the agent,
and every man who has the aspirations of a man, who
is conscious within himself of powers which raise
him above the brute, must exhibit that consciousness
and gratify those aspirations by recognizing the
superior claims of the mind in which they germinate.
" Self-knowledge, self-reverence, self-control, these
three alone lead life to sovereign power." We are
responsible then for our minds, not for their bril-
liancy, not for their power, not for their availability

as instruments of display and personal aggrandizement, but for their use as the gifts of a divine Creator and the representatives of a divine influence in creation and I urge this view the more emphatically on account of the terrible consequences of its neglect. It is strange that men should seem so little aware of the injustice charged against their Maker in their mode of estimating his gifts. Except among a few conscientious thinkers these gifts are claimed and appropriated without hesitation and without acknowledgment, and all the merit and all the glory that can be extracted from their most selfish and despotic use are assumed as the rightful property of the fortunate possessor. But shall we be content with such a view of the being whom in theory, at least, we worship as perfect truth and perfect justice? Is this teeming world, this vast humanity, ushered into existence merely that it may furnish a background for the display of a few lordly intellects or subside into the thraldom of a few despotic wills? Have none but intellectual giants, or those who pass for such, a right to the possession of a thought or the expression of an opinion or the indulgence of a hope? Is it really

so that the great majority of the human race are re-
quired to approach their Maker through the interven-
tion of other minds and to receive the grand but simple truths of existence as they come to them diluted
and disengaged in the crucible of human analysis and
labeled by the endorsement of human authority?
Yet such is and ever has been the human view of the
case. One conspicuous thinker boldly avows the
opinion that the history of human progress resolves
itself into the biography of a few resolute and over-
mastering intellects which have expounded the faith
and controlled the destinies of the age in which they
lived. Here we have, recognized and established, in
the nineteenth century, a system of intellectual despotism for whose political counterpart we must look
among the darkest ages of feudal tyranny. Politi-
cally, we profess to have emancipated ourselves from
these puerilities, but spiritually and intellectually
we still glory in a hero worship only worthy of a bar-
barous apotheosis. I believe that a reaction is inevitable, and that it will exhibit itself in the same disas-
trous results in the world of letters and the world of
thought as have attended the social and political

crises which have convulsed the nations. Much that is noble and beautiful will go down before it, but not to be lost forever, for the plain common sense, the calm second thought of mankind will not forever consent to be sacrificed on the altars of personal ambition. Man will yet learn his true dignity and his true power as " the offspring of God," and will take refuge from ultraisms in the simple conviction that the discovery of truth is the proper employment of mind, and that the noblest intellect is that which most sincerely desires and most thoroughly attains it. Divine truths are simple truths, they are intended to meet the necessities of the human mind wherever and in whatever condition it may be found. In the development and application of these truths it is not intended that we should act as complements to one another ; we cannot be trusted to do so, we are too weak, too ignorant, too easily uplifted by a little comparative activity or precocity of intellect to render such an attitude safe either to him who imparts or to him who receives ; teaching degenerates into dictation, learning sinks into worship. God is the complement, the only complement of man : communion with him is the only nourishment which can give vitality, energy and enlargement to the mind of his creature ; and the feeblest intellect thus vivified and enlarged becomes more available for all the purposes of wise and noble living than the self-reliant profun‧dity of a des Cartes, or the self-exalting ambition of a Buckle or a Compte.

But in order to accomplish this, you and I, my friends, must learn to value our own minds, must show our reverence for the Creator by recognizing and appreciating the grandeur of his work and feeling how utterly we dishonor him, whenever, by any mock-humility, we consent to its degradation. These minds, which God has given us, we must account for, and if from a fancied sense of inferiority or the in-dulgence of a mortified vanity or a reverence for self-constituted authority, we dare to neglect his gift, we have no right to complain if we forfeit it forever.

The man who yields his judgment to anything but honest conviction, the man who suffers himself to be overawed by the pretentions of a domineering intel-lect, has fairly earned his vassalage and must be con-tent henceforth to lose his individuality. We hear a great deal about the retributions of eternity ; but there are none to be dreaded but such as are the result of our own choice and the consequences of our own laches.

Your Maker is your inspirer and your judge, and you will find in him, not only an infallible guide to your duties, but an all-powerful vindicator of your rights.

Men are everywhere alive to their legal and social claims, and are pressing them with a vindictive fury which will retard their progress and recoil upon themselves ; but they seem, almost in the same proportion, dead to their mental and spiritual privileges, and yet it is these last which are most seriously assailed and most worthy of vindication ; take away my property, deprive me of life if you will, but leave my intellect untrammelled, let my spirit go free and it will soon soar out of the reach of earthly chains and human despotism. A great deal of this despotism is perpetrated under cover of an assumed obligation to defend *the truth ;* but this is only another form of presumption. Truth—divine truth—the truth which we need and which alone can correct human folly and promote human expansion, is by no means that feeble and mawkish thing which requires to be sustained upon its pedestal by external supports. Truth, be well assured, can take very good care of herself, she needs no champion and will endure no patronage at human hands, and it will be well for us all, from the highest to the lowest, if we be found walking humbly and carefully in that noble company gathered from the east and from the west, from the north and from the south of every tribe and family and sect and persuasion under heaven, who are content to follow patiently in her footsteps and have resisted the temptation to thrust their insignificance in the path of her resistless and triumphant advance. But again, we are responsible for our virtue, not that negative and imbecile thing which so often claims the title, but that revealed and embodied force which was implied in the original construction of the word and of which the Roman was blindly conscious when he named it "manhood." In our time men have adroitly contrived to turn the tables and virtue, nowadays, is but too apt to degenerate into a meek surrender to evil as a necessary consequence of human imperfection; but I still cleave to the old Roman interpretation, changing only the field of contest; we have reached a stage in earthly progress in which we cannot with much claim to intelligence retain the standards which belonged to the infancy of the human intellect. Now, that we have become men, we must put away childish things, we can no longer tilt at the windmill antagonists of a former generation; the struggle for temporal success and material grandeur and human applause has ceased to occupy the minds and employ the energies of honest and intelligent men; that vulgar struggle has been remitted, as it should be, to the thoughtless and the sensuous, to the narrow-minded and the profane; we have reached a higher platform, from whence we have caught glimpses of real life, and we blush with shame to think of the delusions upon which we have expended our energies and wasted our triumphs. We have learned at last, by sad experience, by mortifying failure, by overwhelming defeat, that, "we wrestle not with flesh and blood," and that we have often been the victims of a sardonic mockery, when we fancied ourselves the heroes of a righteous antagonism. No! let us congratulate ourselves that we

have been introduced into a higher life, and that
while virtue in the abstract is the same noble energy
which the Greek admired and the Roman cultivated,
it is exercised upon a higher plane, with a wider
scope and for a grander result than could have
entered into a mind upon which Christianity had not
shed its divine effulgence. Virtue does not now
mean merely courage, it means patience, it means
humility, it means self-sacrifice, it means not only a
readiness to face death, but a willingness to endure
life, when its zest is gone and its bloom decayed—
that living death which no merely human hero could
for a moment endure.

It still means manhood, but a manhood sustained
and energized by a higher spirit; that divine manhood which meets the threats of usurped authority
with the calm rebuke, "Thou couldst have no power
at all against me except it were given thee from
above."

It is for such a manhood as this that we become
responsible when we profess to have risen above the
childishness, the effeminacy and the brutality which
disgrace our social annals, and which form the ele-

ments of every nature in which a divine energy is
not predominant.

Finally, we are responsible for our honor, and here
again I must discriminate ; I do not mean reputation,
nor do I mean homage, nor do I mean popularity ;
these things are external, ambiguous and beyond our
control, they depend upon the passions, the interests
and the caprices of men, they may be unworthily ac-
corded and unjustly withheld, an accident may confer,
a falsehood may withdraw them ; the honor of which
I speak and to which I would direct your ambition
is something very different from these, it is a principle, an internal unchangeable principle; it cannot
be imparted, and it cannot be withheld ; it depends
upon no contingencies ; it is unmoved by threats
and inaccessible to flattery; it is the same lofty
energy in adversity as it is in prosperity; it is as
noble and self-respectful in obscurity as it is modest
and unassuming before the public gaze; it does
not ask what is convenient or what is profit-
able or what is politic, but it rests immovably
upon what is true, what is noble, what is generous,
what is brave ; it is not a relative but an absolute

constituent; it has no envies, no malignities, no hates and no fears; it cannot build itself upon the ruin of another, because it is pledged to consult the feelings and respect the rights and acknowledge the virtues of all with whom it comes in contact; and it is unsuspicious because it is conscious of an energy within which sets at defiance all the powers of darkness. In its social exercise it recognizes no legitimate ground of enmity, but, if an issue is forced upon it, it accepts it reluctantly and allows no personal feeling to degrade the contest; seeking only the truth it discards all irrelevant and *ad captandum* influences, scorns all mean advantage and welcomes defeat in a wrong cause. It meets its adversary face to face, not seeking victory, but right, and never feels itself stronger or higher than when it has confessed a wrong or redressed an injury.

I have been at the pains thus to analyze and define because a principle is current in the world which, under the name of honor and with professions and claims which attract the thoughtless and deceive the unwary, oppresses society by an influence the very reverse of that I have endeavored to invoke, an influence which narrows the mind, corrupts the heart, degrades the spirit and brutalizes the manners of all who yield to its irrational control. I wish to relieve you, as far as I can, from entering upon the exacting duties of life burdened with an incubus which will utterly unfit you for their proper performance; you cannot defend your honor, its proper function is to defend you, and if you have been so unfortunate as to cultivate a sickly sentimentality instead of a robust and manly power, the sooner you correct the error the better will it be for your manhood and your true success: depend upon it, the only honor that is worth cultivating is that which can take care of itself, which is strong and true and trustful and patient, willing and able to bide its time; that honor which must be guarded with jealous watchfulness, which cannot endure a *slur*, which must be kept clean by blood, is not honor, but its shadow reputation, and you may well be anxious about that, for its very existence depends upon the sunshine of prosperity.

And now you will charge me, very justly, with presenting you an impracticable, a superhuman standard. I acknowledge that I have done so, and that I am

4

bound in consequence, not to close this address until I have suggested some reasonable ground for the injustice and some adequate provision for the difficulty in which I seem to have involved you ; fortunately I have not far to go ; the very nature of the difficulty suggests the remedy : If the work is superhuman so must be the agent, and you are privileged to claim an interposition adequate to your necessities ; you cannot rise above yourselves ; you cannot give more than you have received or live in an atmosphere unsuited to your organs of respiration ; God is not unjust and we are authorized to assume all that logically follows from that inevitable postulate ; if he requires virtue above your strength, His strength must be pledged to aid you in the attainment ; here lies the secret of your paradoxical experience ; you must invoke and exercise a superhuman, a divine power, and upon that power you must cast the burden of your superhuman responsibilities.

It is needless to enlarge upon this suggestion, it commends itself to the intelligence of every mind capable of appreciating its own native dignity and ultimate destiny.

THE PATHOS OF POETRY.

HEN the great English Epic evolved line by
    line
    From the mind of the hermit we now call
divine,
And the whole stately structure was reared in its
    place
Resplendent with genius and instinct with grace,
The soul from whose throes came that marvelous
    birth
In its struggle for truth had been crushed to the
    Earth ;
And there as he pondered, deserted, forlorn,
The Sectary's hate and the Courtier's scorn,
From the depths of his time-darkened spirit there
    sprung
That song which no time-nurtured bard could have
    sung ;
The sunlight, withdrawn from those fathomless eyes,
Rose cloudless and warm in unchangable skies ;

And the darkness which curtained his earth-bounded
    sight,
Gave relief to those visions of heavenly light,
Which, nurtured in sorrow and tempered by pain,
Revealed to his soul how his loss might be gain.

The Garden of Eden, the home of the soul,
Whose denizens felt not and feared not control ;
The birth place of innocence, cradled in sense,
Unconscious of virtue, unknowing offence,
Unfallen, and therefore unable to rise,
Never touching the depths, never reaching the skies ;
The womb of creation from whence she might spring
Into finite existence, an objective thing,
In that gorgeous, phenomenal mystery draped,
The reflex of mind in whose mold it was shaped ;
And shrouding the sensitive creature from ill
While soft to the touch of an infinite will.
The life-tree that nourished, the death-tree that
    warned,
The tempter that blasted what God had adorned,
The perennial grove and the amaranth bower,
The fountain that watered the tree and the flower,

All rose at the touch of his life-giving wand
Embodied his thought and fulfilled his command ;
And the pictures which sprang from the touch of the
      blind,
Still ravish the sight and the soul of mankind.

He stands not alone, down the broad aisle of time
Far off in the distance, majestic, sublime,
Stands the bard of the Ages, whose voice evermore
Shall ring through the arches of time as of yore
And in echo still clear and sonorous restore
The song of the free to each freedomless shore.

From the primeval dawn of man's earliest thought
When pure from it's spring inspiration was caught,
All nature was vital with marks of its God
And man found his Maker wherever he trod :
He dwelt on the mountain in lordly conclave,
He hallowed the forest and brightened the wave,
To furnish his weapon the sun lent his beam
And the naiad confessed his abode in the stream.
One divinity guided the steeds of the sun
And another presided when daylight was done,

And thus the poor heir of ephemeral day
Surmounted in spirit his vesture of clay.
The thought of the seer was narrow and crude,
The form of his mythos was simple and rude ;
But his ear was attuned to æonian sounds,
And unconsciously spurned it's material bounds.
But Olympus no longer can shelter the Gods,
Earth trembles no longer when Jupiter nods,
And the chain he suspended from heaven to earth,
No longer avails to demonstrate his worth ;
Yet the Father we crave and the God we adore
Bends over his children in love, as of yore ;
And the Power diffracted by myopic eyes
Now shines as a unit direct from the skies.

Creation can never Creator disown,
God moves in the water and rests in the stone,
And the Pagan who saw him in mountain and stream
Shames the victim of science who counts him a dream ;
And scorns the transcendent devotion refined,
Which excogitates God from the depths of the mind
A subjective God whose enjoyment depends
On submission enforced to his personal ends ;

An irrational God whose omnipotent will
Draws a meaningless line twixt the good and the ill ;
A tyrannous God whose despotic command
Creates for destruction the work of his hand,
Almighty to punish the thrall's of his hate
Omniscient to cognize, in foresight, their fate.
Far better the poet who saw him afar,
And worshipped his God in the sun or the star,
Than the Zealot who makes him the tool of his spite
Or the Bigot who finites his infinite light.
One Father we have, the protector of all,
Who masters the great and ennobles the small ;
What he has created in vain we despise,
Not an atom too small for his vigilant eyes ;
And the mortal, who dares to interpret his plan,
Needs the mind and the heart of an infinite man.
The sensual thought, whether gross or refined,
Is the herald of death to the sensual mind ;
And the fruit of that tree, ever fair to the sight
Is poison to him who partakes not aright ;
Time and space are but " thought forms " of sensual
        man,
There was never a time when creation began ;

And thought cannot find in indefinite space,
The outcome of might which no thought can embrace.
All hail! then, the Poet, whose songs interfuse
A Power divine in his mythical muse;
And mingle the tones of conventional thought,
With a waft of the air from eternity brought.

There's a darkness excluding the sensual light,
Sternly hiding creation from visual light,
Reducing the splendors of nature to naught
And compelling the mind to intuitive thought.
There's a darkness involving a murkier gloom,
The darkness of death which o'ershadows the tomb;
And the ray, which can pierce through that opaline
        shade,
Must be lit in the land where the lights never fade.
The Poet, who stands twixt the living and dead,
The light of whose life has been quenched in the bed
Where the form which was hallowed by friendship is
        cold,
And the earth which was vital is turning to mold;
The Poet whose innermost light has gone out
In the coldness of death and the darkness of doubt,

Must illumine his soul with the sunlight of trust,
Ere his spirit can wake from its sleep in the dust.
And *the Laureate*, who reared o'er the grave of his
    friend
A memento whose pathos time never can mend,
Has hallowed the ground where his footsteps have trod
And pointed the pathway from nature to God.
Ah! deep is the vale of the shadow of death,
And prostrate the soul that has wandered from faith ;
And dread, in the darkness, the cry of despair,
Which is wrung from that soul in its midnight of
    fear ;
But the spark of divinity never goes out,
And the mind where it rests cannot linger in doubt
And "*resurgam*" is written in letters of light,
On the crest of the mortal who stands in the fight,
The good fight of faith, the internal strife,
Which triumphs in death and which issues in life.

It is strange, it is wonderful, minstrels that sing
In the power of sunlight and glory of spring,
Never touch the true heart of humanity so
As the Poet who labors in darkness and woe :

Like the artist who shrouds the beholder in gloom
And curtains the window and darkens the room,
And woos, to illustrate the child of his heart,
Concentrated light to emblazon his art,
Or astronomer, sounding the depths of the sky,
Through a tunnel of darkness brings light to his
     eye,
So the Poet, whose vision to nature is blind,
Sees a loftier world with the eye of his mind,
And dying to sense and forgetful of time,
Awakens, *resurgent*, to visions sublime.

The Bards of the Ages!   The finger of time,
As it sweeps o'er the dial in movement sublime,
Marks the epochs which signal it's awful advance,
By chimings which waken the ear they entrance ;
And those watchmen who stand, each alone, on his
     tower
Give note to the slumbering world, of the hour,
Now loud, as in triumph, now low, as in fear,
Now warning the sleeper when danger is near ;
Each looking above for the keynote to give
Inspiration to song and the power to live ;

Each looking within for the soul to reply
To the touch of the magnet that draws him on high.

We live in two worlds, the philosophers teach,
And science concurs in her technical speech,
And Poets give rythmical note of the fact,
And heroes respond in superlative act.
But Philosophy fails to illustrate her creed,
And Science supplies not the clue that we need ;
And the World of the Poet, subjective alone,
Only claims the ideal and vague as its own.
Action only is real, the issue that springs
From the marriage of thought with phenomenal things,
The potential evolved into actual life
By the fusion of elements singly at strife.
From the world of the senses and world of the mind
Antithetic in nature and different in kind,
There emerge into action spontaneous and free,
Individual spirits of lofty degree ;
And nature, which seems universal in plan,
Attains the responsible unit in man :
A unit endowed with a glorious dower,
A selfhood instinct with appropriate power,

A form which embodies an infinite life,
Giving light to its darkness and strength to its strife;
A form, in which Godhead and manhood combine
To embody forever the human divine :
A Temple whose curtains but faintly conceal
The shrine which the *Holiest* came to reveal ;
Drawing up to himself by an infinite art
The spirit enthralled by its earthlier part.
Then man becomes Godlike, when God becomes man.
And here, on this earth, is developed the plan
Which satisfies thought and reconciles doubt
And unifies all things, within and without;
And thus from the mist of the mythical ages
Recorded by Bards and embalmed by the sages,
Through the long-drawn and teeming succession of
          years
Polluted by crimes and embittered by tears,
Those types of the Godlike, exalted and free,
Foreshadow the glories which yet are to be;
Those types of the Godlike, to worldlings unknown,
Who leaven the world by their presence alone,
Who stand in their lot, representative men,
Bravely making their mark with their blood or their pen:

Responsible each for his act and his thought
With a mind unseduced and a conscience unbought ;
Who live for their manhood and dare to be free
Where the thralls of the world bow idolatrous knee.

Our life is no drama, no scenic display—
Now tragic, now comic, then passing away ;
With selfhood comes conscience and conscience sub-
       tends
An infinite presence and infinite ends ;
The power of choice, which ennobles our life,
Gives token within of an infinite strife ;
And he only conquers whose triumph proclaims
A struggle inspired by infinite aims ;
No contest with man, no irrational strife,
With ills which beset our external life ;
No wasting of energy, misuse of power,
In impotent strife with the wrongs of the hour ;
No weak prostitution of mental resource,
In subtle refinement or pompous discourse ;
Abusing the power which language supplies
For a vulgar renown which the noble despise ;

Disgusting the honest, misleading the blind
And only deceiving the cultureless mind.
No pitiful struggle for place or for name.
The paltry result of an ignoble game ;
But the God-like employment of God-given mind
In loving and raising and blessing mankind ;
Magnanimous thought for the good of the whole
In noble response for the gift of a soul ;
And self with the falsehood in which it reposed
By the might of true manhood forever deposed.

Imprisoned in sense as the bird in its shell
We live, all unconscious, the thralls of a spell
Whose glamor avails to conceal from the mind
That its thought is unformed and its vision purblind,
That the world of true being, from which it is barred,
Is hedged by the sword of the seraph on guard,
And that all that the effort of man can achieve
Is, Creation accomplished, its cause to believe.
When worldings paint heaven, they travesty earth
Unlearned in the lore of the spirit's new birth ;
A sensual heaven, with worldly delights
And melodious sounds and enrapturing sights ;

Where the body set free from the safeguards of
    earth,
Shall wallow in pleasure and revel in mirth ;
Where the unfettered passions, released from control,
Shall return to their house in the regarnished soul.
And fiends of ambition and demons of vice,
Hold revelry high in a fool's paradise.
But Heaven dwells not in the sensual mind,
Whether lofty or low, whether gross or refined ;
It knows not the limits of time or of space,
Is heedless of years and unmindful of place ;
It's infinite home is the bosom of love,
Contracted below, but expanded above ;
And wherever the spirit of charity reigns,
Eternity measures the life it maintains ;
The malice of man cannot banish it thence,
It defies all the blundering weapons of sense,
Whose keenness controlled by the hand of a friend,
Is directed alone to arouse and amend,
It heeds not the agent, or only to bless,
Despises revenge and is cold to redress ;
But awaits, in the calm of ineffable peace,
The summons which heralds the spirit's release.

We are creatures of time and we live in a zone
Whose orbit is scanned by the Maker alone ;
The impotent tools of omnipotent mind,
Who work in time's loom unconsulted and blind :
The ignorant agents of wisdom supreme,
Borne ruthlessly onward by time's ceaseless stream ;
Who shape not events, nor control their estate,
But live at the mercy of merciless fate.
The machine of creation in perfect accord,
Unceasingly prints an unchangeable word,
Which stamped on the organ of changeable man,
Results in the chaos in which time began ;
But creation, the work of an infinite hand
Permits no free agent to cross his command
And the gift of a *will*, introactive alone
Involves not the *power* to alter a stone :
Affects not creation, but only is given
To locate the agent in Hell or in Heaven.
In the pride of our selfhood we thoughtlessly deem
Things are in reality such as they seem ;
But logic, too stern for unreasoning man,
Incontestably proves an unchangeable plan.

In a world of perfection an atom astray
Brings ruin as sure as the failure of day,
And what must ensue if the thoughtless and blind
Interfere with the order of infinite mind ?
Thou thrall of probation relentlessly tried,
By visions of beauty forever denied,
Who livest for duty nor seekest reward,
And holdest thy standard direct from the Lord ;
Whose aims are misjudged by a sensual age,
And whose name finds no place upon history's page,
Thou thrall of probation ! be still of good cheer,
Before the Unerring, thy record is clear ;
Enough that the issue for which thou hast striven
Shall find its due place in the archives of Heaven ;
And the crown now denied thee or given in scorn,
Shall rest on thy brow, dispossessed of its thorn ;
Enough that the stone which the builders denied,
Shall stand in its corner, its claim justified ;
And the workman withdrawn from his labor of love,
Shall find never ending employment above.

Our natures are two-fold, without and within,
Are the parts of the synthesis whence we begin ;

5

And mind with its analogue matter compose
The ultimate ovum from whence man arose.
Mind alone is not man, unconscious and vain
It wanders unformed till a body it gain ;
 Then the composite being, who dominates earth,
 Takes his place as ordained at his wonderful
          birth ;
And when thus the concrete individual gains
The conscious existence which henceforth remains,
He finds now within him, aside from his will,
A responsible claim he can never fulfil ;
And, urged by a pressure beyond his control,
Appropriates evil as part of his soul.
Thus the conflict begins, to surcease nevermore,
Till his destiny point to that ultimate shore
Where the claims of probation are finally weighed,
 And fixed by the choice each probationer made ;
When, its first combination resolved once again
Into separate elements, pure and inane ;
The spirit of life, its identity lost,
A naked, unconscious, unrecognized ghost,
Attains the objective and conscious once more
By fusion with substance eternally pure,

And the self which once crept as a mortal on earth,
Rejoices on high in a heavenly birth.
There pure and serene, in eternal embrace,
Exalted in nature and perfect in grace,
The Psyche which chafed under secular vows
Shall repose in the arms of a heavenly spouse,
And the voices which welcome her advent above
Shall hail her, the bride of an infinite love.

www.ingramcontent.com/pod-product-compliance
Lightning Source LLC
Chambersburg PA
CBHW021628270326
41931CB00008B/928